W9-CAW-087

MAJOR EUROPEAN UNION NATIONS

Austria
Belgium
Czech Republic
Denmark
France
Germany
Greece
Ireland

Italy
The Netherlands
Poland
Portugal
Spain
Sweden
United Kingdom

Major European Union Nations

DENMARK

by
Heather Docalavich and Shaina C. Indovino

Mason Crest

Mason Crest
370 Reed Road, Broomall,
Pennsylvania 19008
www.masoncrest.com

Printed in the Hashemite Kingdom of Jordan.

First printing
9 8 7 6 5 4 3 2 1

Library of Congress Cataloging-in-Publication Data

Docalavich, Heather.
  Denmark / by Heather Docalavich and Shaina C. Indovino.
      p. cm. — (The European Union : political, social, and economic cooperation)
  Includes bibliographical references and index.
  ISBN 978-1-4222-2238-6 (hardcover) — ISBN 978-1-4222-2231-7 (series hardcover) — ISBN 978-1-4222-9265-5 (ebook)
  1. Denmark—Juvenile literature. 2. European Union—Denmark—Juvenile literature. I. Indovino, Shaina Carmel. II. Title.
  DL109.D63 2012
  948.9—dc22
                                          2010051090

Produced by Harding House Publishing Services, Inc.
www.hardinghousepages.com
Interior layout by Micaela Sanna.
Cover design by Torque Advertising + Design.

Contents

Introduction 8

1. Modern Issues 11

2. Denmark's History and Government 25

3. The Economy 37

4. Denmark's People and Culture 45

5. Looking to the Future 53

Time Line 56

Further Reading/Internet Resources 57

For More Information 58

Glossary 59

Index 62

Picture Credits 63

About the Authors and the Consultant 64

DENMARK
European Union Member since 1973

Frederikshavn
Hjørring
Brønderslev
Ålborg

Lemvig
Viborg
Randers
Holsterbro

Ringkøbing
Hering
Årbus
Helsingør

Horsens

Veile
Fredericia
Copenhagen
Frederiksberg
Esbjerg
Kolding
Ribe
Odense
Slagelse
Haderslev
Nœstved
Svenborg
Sønderborg
Nykobing

INTRODUCTION

Sixty years ago, Europe lay scarred from the battles of the Second World War. During the next several years, a plan began to take shape that would unite the countries of the European continent so that future wars would be inconceivable. On May 9, 1950, French Foreign Minister Robert Schuman issued a declaration calling on France, Germany, and other European countries to pool together their coal and steel production as "the first concrete foundation of a European federation." "Europe Day" is celebrated each year on May 9 to commemorate the beginning of the European Union (EU).

The EU consists of twenty-seven countries, spanning the continent from Ireland in the west to the border of Russia in the east. Eight of the ten most recently admitted EU member states are former communist regimes that were behind the Iron Curtain for most of the latter half of the twentieth century.

Any European country with a democratic government, a functioning market economy, respect for fundamental rights, and a government capable of implementing EU laws and policies may apply for membership. Bulgaria and Romania joined the EU in 2007. Croatia, Serbia, Turkey, Iceland, Montenegro, and Macedonia have also embarked on the road to EU membership.

While the EU began as an idea to ensure peace in Europe through interconnected economies, it has evolved into so much more today:

- Citizens can travel freely throughout most of the EU without carrying a passport and without stopping for border checks.

- EU citizens can live, work, study, and retire in another EU country if they wish.

- The euro, the single currency accepted throughout seventeen of the EU countries (with more to come), is one of the EU's most tangible achievements, facilitating commerce and making possible a single financial market that benefits both individuals and businesses.

- The EU ensures cooperation in the fight against cross-border crime and terrorism.

- The EU is spearheading world efforts to preserve the environment.

- As the world's largest trading bloc, the EU uses its influence to promote fair rules for world trade, ensuring that globalization also benefits the poorest countries.

- The EU is already the world's largest donor of humanitarian aid and development assistance, providing around 60 percent of global official development assistance to developing countries in 2011.

The EU is not a nation intended to replace existing nations. The EU is unique—its member countries have established common institutions to which they delegate some of their sovereignty so that decisions on matters of joint interest can be made democratically at the European level.

Europe is a continent with many different traditions and languages, but with shared values such as democracy, freedom, and social justice, cherished values well known to North Americans. Indeed, the EU motto is "United in Diversity."

Enjoy your reading. Take advantage of this chance to learn more about Europe and the EU!

Ambassador John Bruton,
Former EU President and Prime Minister of Ireland

Christianshavns Kanal in Copenhagen, Denmark.

CHAPTER 1

MODERN ISSUES

Denmark is a generally peaceful country. The Danes are known for staying out of trouble unless it knocks on their doorstep. From the beginning, however, they realized how important it was to become involved in coalition movements throughout Europe. But even as loyal members of the European Union, the Danes were reluctant to adopt certain EU policies. This included accepting EU citizenship and a common currency (the euro).

Despite this, the Danes are extremely supportive of the European Union when dealing with issues outside Denmark's borders. The Danes maintain good relations with their geographical neighbors, and they offer assistance to developing nations. In fact, Denmark is one of the only countries to exceed the UN goal of contribution to these nations. Denmark has also sent military assistance to areas that need it most, such as Kosovo and Afghanistan. The Danes have played a leadership role in helping Eastern European countries make a smooth transition into the European Union.

In other words, the Danish people are more than happy to help out with world affairs—but they do not want too many restrictions placed on them within their own borders. The question of "how much involvement is too much?" is still a big concern to Danes. As the world becomes more globally integrated, the Danes must make important choices. How much do they want to allow their country to be influenced by the rest of the world? And how much will they allow the EU to shape their policies toward the rest of the world?

TENSIONS WITH MUSLIMS

The Muslim presence in Denmark is an area where the Danes are struggling to resolve these questions. Despite being on the northern border of

Flags of the European Union.

The Formation of the European Union

The EU is a confederation of European nations that continues to grow. All countries that enter the EU agree to follow common laws about foreign security policies. They also agree to cooperate on legal matters that go on within the EU. The European Council meets to discuss all international matters and make decisions about them. Each country's own concerns and interests are important, though. And apart from legal and financial issues, the EU tries to uphold values such as peace and solidarity, human dignity, freedom, and equality. All member countries remain autonomous. This means that they generally keep their own laws and regulations. The EU becomes involved only if there is an international issue or if a member country has violated the principles of the union.

The idea for a union among European nations was first mentioned after World War II. The war had devastated much of Europe, both physically and financially. In 1950, French foreign minister Robert Schuman suggested that France and West Germany combine their coal and steel industries under one authority. Both countries would have control over the industries. This would help them become more financially stable. It would also make war between the countries much more difficult. The idea was interesting to other European countries as well. In 1951, France, West Germany, Belgium, Luxembourg, the Netherlands, and Italy signed the Treaty of Paris, creating the European Coal and Steel Community. These six countries would become the core of the EU.

In 1957, these same countries signed the Treaties of Rome, creating the European Economic Community. This combined their economies into a single European economy. In 1965, the Merger Treaty brought together a number of these treaty organizations. The organizations were joined under a common banner, known as the European Community. Finally, in 1992, the Maastricht Treaty was signed. This treaty defined the European Union. It gave a framework for expanding the EU's political role, particularly in the area of foreign and security policy. It would also replace national currencies with the euro. The next year, the treaty went into effect. At that time, the member countries included the original six plus another six who had joined during the 1970s and '80s.

In the following years, the EU would take more steps to form a single market for its members. This would make joining the union even more of an advantage. Three more countries joined during the 1990s. Another twelve joined in the first decade of the twenty-first century. As of 2012, six countries were waiting to join the EU.

Muslims in the European Union

Muslims are people who follow Islam, a religion that grew from some of the same roots as Judaism and Christianity. "Islam" means "submission to God," and Muslims try to let God shape all aspects of their lives. They refer to God as Allah; their holy scriptures are called the Qur'an, and they consider the Prophet Muhammad to be their greatest teacher.

About 16 million Muslims live in the European Union—but their stories vary from country to country. Some Muslim populations have been living in Europe for hundreds of years. Others came in the middle of the twentieth century. Still others are recent refugees from the troubled Middle East. By 2020, the Muslim population in Europe is predicted to double. By 2050, one in five Europeans are likely to be Muslim, and by 2100, Muslims may make up one-quarter of Europe's people.

Not all Europeans are happy about these predictions. Negative stereotypes about Muslims are common in many EU countries. Some Europeans think all Muslims are terrorists. But stereotypes are dangerous!

When you believe a stereotype, you think that people in a certain group all act a certain way. "All jocks are dumb" is a stereotype. "All women are emotional" is another stereotype, and another is, "All little boys are rough and noisy." Stereotypes aren't true! And when we use stereotypes to think about others, we often fall into prejudice—thinking that some groups of people aren't as good as others.

Fundamentalist Muslims want to get back to the fundamentals—the basics—of Islam. However, their definition of what's "fundamental" is not always the same as other Muslims'. Generally speaking, they are afraid that the influence of Western morals and values will be bad for Muslims. They believe that the laws of Islam's holy books should be followed literally. Many times, they are willing to kill for their beliefs—and they are often willing to die for them as well. Men and women who are passionate about these beliefs have taken part in violent attacks against Europe and the United States. They believe that terrorism will make the world take notice of them, that it will help them fight back against the West's power.

But most Muslims are not terrorists. In fact, most Muslims are law-abiding and hardworking citizens of the countries where they live. Some Muslims, however, believe that women should have few of the rights that women expect in most countries of the EU. This difference creates tension, since the EU guarantees women the same rights as men.

But not all Muslims are so conservative and strict. Many of them believe in the same "golden rule" preached by all major religions: "Treat everyone the way you want to be treated."

But despite this, hate crimes against Muslims are increasing across the EU. These crimes range from death threats and murder to more minor assaults, such as spitting and name-calling. Racism against Muslims is a major problem in many parts of the EU. The people of the European Union must come to terms with the fact that Muslims are a part of them now. Terrorism is the enemy to be fought—not Muslims.

Europe, far away from recent military conflicts, Denmark has seen its fair share of tension over Islamic issues. In 2005, a Danish newspaper printed a series of controversial cartoon showing Mohammed, the sacred prophet of the Islamic faith.

According to Muslim belief, Mohammed should never be depicted in any form, good or bad. By creating a cartoon showing the Prophet, the Danish were insulting those of Islamic heritage. Even worse, they were committing sacrilege. Muslims around the world were furious.

Muslims burned Danish flags. In February 2006, Muslims marched outside the Danish Embassy in London. In Norway, 1,000 Muslims cab drivers stopped driving. A Catholic priest was

Activists protest against anti-Muslim campaigners in Aarhus, Denmark.

killed in Turkey. In 2008, the authorities in Belarus jailed an editor for publishing the cartoons. And the anger kept simmering. In September 2010, a Muslim was injured while making a bomb he planned to detonate in Copenhagen, Denmark's capital city, to retaliate against the newspaper. In December 2010, the Danish authorities arrested four Muslims before they could murder the staff of the newspaper that originally printed the cartoons.

Many non-Muslims insist it's an issue of free speech, that Muslim **radicals** are opposed to the **democratic** principle that gives newspapers the right to print whatever they want. After all, Danes pride themselves on their tolerance and respect for others.

But some Danes see the situation differently. They say that the publication of the cartoons was never intended to trigger a debate about freedom of expression. Instead, they say that the cartoons' publication was just one obvious example of the general hostility toward anything Muslim that exists in Denmark.

A few decades ago, Denmark had no Muslims at all. Today, there are more than 200,000 Muslims in Denmark, a country with a population of more than 5 million. Many Danes see Muslim immigrants as a threat to the survival of Danish culture.

This hostility is demonstrated in various ways. Muslims cannot build mosques in Copenhagen. Denmark has no Muslim cemeteries, so the bodies of Muslims have to be flown back to their home countries for proper burial. In 2006, the Danish minister for cultural affairs asked scholars, artists, and writers to create a collection of Danish art, music, literature, and film. The minister of cultural affairs revealed that he wanted "to create a last line of defense against the influence of Islam in Denmark." He said, "In Denmark we have seen the appearance of a parallel society in which minorities practice their own medieval values and undemocratic views. This is the new front in our cultural war."

When the Danish flag was burned in Arab countries, the reaction in Denmark was outrage. Many people stood behind the newspaper that had printed the cartoon. Political parties against immigration gained power. Newspapers and Danish citizens insisted that any Danish Muslim who protested against the cartoon should have their status as citizens examined.

Others, however, say that the Muslim leaders and their followers simply ran out of options. They had tried to get the Danish newspaper to recognize its offense and apologize. They tried to enlist the support of the government. They asked a local prosecutor to file suit under the country's blasphemy law. And they asked ambassadors in Denmark from Muslim countries to meet with the Danish prime minister. These were all perfectly legal and peaceful measures to take—but the Muslim leaders got nowhere. No one would listen to them or take them seriously. So they were frustrated. They turned to more violent measures.

Violence is never a good answer. But an atmosphere of **prejudice** and **discrimination** breeds anger—and all too often anger breeds violence.

Gypsy children in a train station.

THE ROMA

Muslims are not the only group of people who face discrimination and prejudice in Denmark. The Roma—also known as Gypsies—also encounter similar problems.

The first Gypsies in Denmark came from Scotland and Germany in 1505. From then on, Danish authorities made sporadic efforts to drive them out of Denmark. In the nineteenth century, the laws against Gypsies eased for a few years, only to

Who Are the Roma?

About a thousand years ago, groups of people migrated from northern India, spreading across Europe over the next several centuries. Though these people actually came from several different tribes (the largest of which were the Sinti and Roma), the people of Europe called them simply "Gypsies"—a shortened version of "Egyptians," since people thought they came from Egypt.

Europeans were frightened of these dark-skinned, non-Christian people who spoke a foreign language. Unlike the settled people of Europe, the Roma were wanderers, with no ties to the land. Europeans did not understand them. Stories and stereotypes grew up about the Gypsies, and these fanned the flames of prejudice and discrimination. Many of these same stories and stereotypes are still believed today.

Throughout the centuries, non-Gypsies continually tried to either assimilate the Gypsies or kill them. Attempts to assimilate the Gypsies involved stealing their children and placing them with other families; giving them cattle and feed, expecting them to become farmers; outlawing their customs, language, and clothing, and forcing them to attend school and church. In many ways the Roma of Europe were treated much as the European settlers treated the Native peoples of North America.

Many European laws allowed—or even commanded—the killing of Gypsies. A practice of "Gypsy hunting"—similar to fox hunting—was both common and legal in some parts of Europe. Even as late as 1835, a Gypsy hunt in Denmark "brought in a bag of over 260 men, women, and children." But the worst of all crimes against the Roma happened in the twentieth century, when Hitler's Third Reich sent them to concentration camps. As many as half a million Gypsies died in the Nazis' death camps.

be put in place again at the beginning of the twentieth century. A national police force drove out most of the Roma from Denmark by 1939. Then, in 1953, a few Roma immigrated from Eastern and Central Europe.

When Denmark joined the EU, however, this meant that immigrants could enter freely from other member nations, allowing the Roma to once more enter Denmark in greater numbers. Many Danes were not happy about this.

An incident in the summer of 2010 revealed the growing tension between the Roma and the Danish government, when twenty-three EU citizens of Roma descent were arrested and deported from Denmark. The arrests were made immediately after the mayor of Copenhagen had called on the Danish government to adopt measures to rid Copenhagen of "criminal Roma." The Danish minister of justice immediately took action, though no investigation was made nor were the individuals ever legally convicted of the alleged thefts. In response, Roma organizations spoke out, asking that the Danish government ensure that there would be no further arrests of Roma without evidence or legal proceedings. The EU's Freedom of Movement Directive guarantees all residents of the

Painting by William-Adolphe Bouguereau of two Gypsy girls. Titled *Jeunes Bohemiennes*, or Young Gypsies.

Copenhagen, Denmark

European Union certain immigration rights, and the Danish government had gone against this law. The Roma groups also asked that in the future Danish officials would refrain from making racist or **inflammatory** statements against the Roma in Denmark.

IMMIGRATION

Both the Muslim and Roma issues have to do with another ongoing issue in Denmark: immigration. The EU allows all EU citizens to move freely across national borders—but with so many new nations entering the EU, this means that more and more people can move unchecked around Europe. This has become a major problem in the eyes of many Western European countries, including Denmark.

In 2010, the Danish government came up with an idea to tighten immigration rules using a points system that would reflect the immigrants' desirability, based on education, work experience, and language skills. Even foreigners who are married to Danish citizens and want residency in Denmark will have to accumulate points. Denmark already has one of Europe's toughest stances on immigration, and immigration laws look to become even stricter.

WHO HAS THE POWER?

One of the big issues in the EU is similar to one that the United States faces as well: who should have more power, the central government (the EU in Europe, or the Federal Government in Washington, D.C., in the United States) or the individual members (the nations of Europe or the states of the United States)? This issue becomes obvious when smaller issues arise. In the United

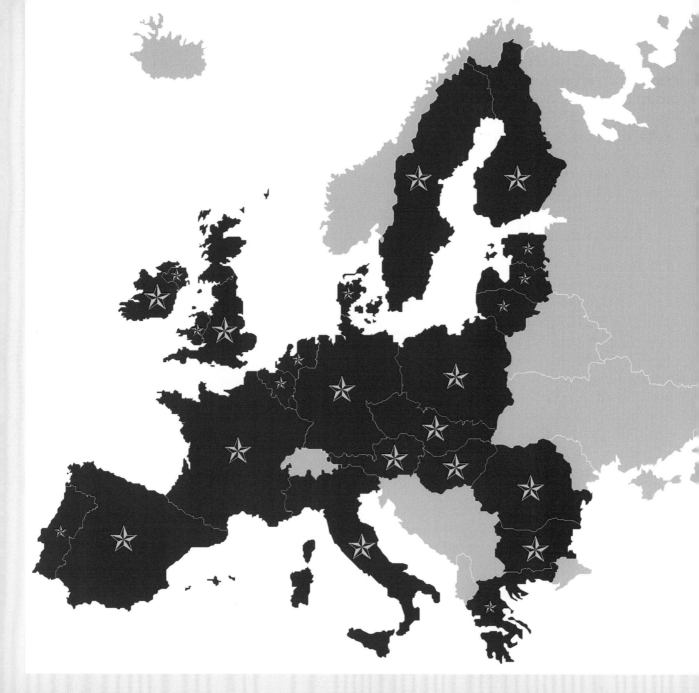

One issue the European Union faces is who should have the most power—the central government, or each individual nation.

States, it came to a head in the 1800s over the issue of slavery, causing the Civil War, but it continues to be an important question whenever states don't agree on a particular issue, such as same-sex marriage or abortion rights. The individual issues in Europe are different (they often have to do with immigration and with money), but the big issue is very much the same. Will the EU be able to unite its power the way the United States did—or will it continue to act as separate nations?

Kronborg Castle (Hamlet's Castle) in Helsingor

2 Denmark's History and Government

Denmark has a rich and ancient history. For the Danes, the continuity of their language, history, and culture is a source of pride and the basis for their strong sense of national identity. In modern times, Denmark stands as a strong, **democratic** country, a prominent member of the United Nations, and a central figure in the EU.

As a nation, Denmark is committed to peace and shares good relations with other countries. The Danish people are equally proud of their history and the way in which their small country has embraced the changes that the twenty-first century has brought.

DENMARK IN ANCIENT TIMES

Five thousand years ago, most of the inhabitants of Danish lands made their home near the coast and lived on fish and shellfish. They supplemented their diet by hunting seals and other game, which provided skins for clothing and shelter as well as food. In those times, a dense forest blanketed most of the countryside.

The earliest people of Denmark worshiped the ancient **pagan** gods, and when an important chief passed away, he was laid to rest in a burial mound, together with his slaves, animals, wives, and other belongings. In modern times, these graves have been found scattered around the country, and by carefully studying their contents, researchers have been able to piece together many details of the daily lives of these ancient people. A few bodies have been found mummified in **bogs**, so we know a great deal about how these people looked, how they dressed, and even what they ate.

Around 500 CE, a tribe calling itself the Danes migrated from Sweden with the intent of conquering what is now Denmark. Their language, preserved in a few ancient writings, was a northern German dialect, which already featured many important differences from German itself. Modern Danish is very different from both Swedish and German in tone and spelling, although enough similarities exist for most Danes to understand Swedish.

In Germany, to the south, the Franks emerged as the most powerful tribe in the region. Charlemagne, a Frank and the greatest ruler of the era, built an empire that extended over Germany, France, and much of central Italy. The Franks began to push north, hoping to further expand their holdings. Around 800 CE, the Danish Viking Godfred took up the challenge posed by the Franks and established the boundaries of his country, now known as Denmark. Over the next three hundred years, Vikings would play a prominent role in many of the most important and dramatic events in European history.

THE AGE OF THE VIKINGS

The bold Vikings ruled the North and Baltic seas, and the continental rivers adjacent to them, for long periods. Known for their sense of adventure and lack of fear, the Vikings were some of Europe's earliest explorers. On one of their trips they even visited North America, hundreds of years before a similar journey would make Christopher Columbus famous. Several Danish towns that began as Viking settlements are now over one thousand years old. Copenhagen, the Danish capital, which started out as a small fishing village with some traders and a marketplace, was founded more than eight hundred years ago.

Technologically, the Vikings had a great advantage over the other people of that time, namely their fast, seaworthy warships. With their open, square-rigged vessels, the Vikings sailed Europe's coastal waters, acting as traders, pirates, and colonizers. Coastal monasteries and abbeys lived in fear of attack from these pagan seafarers who did

Viking graveyard at Lindholm Hoje in Denmark

Queen's lifetime guards

not hesitate to raid Christian houses of worship for valuable gold and silver. The word Viking, which means "one who fights at sea," can be found on several **runic** stones from that period.

Initially, Vikings operated as a loosely united set of tribes, with authority in the hands of one chief or another. However, by 900 CE, Denmark was united under the rule of one king. King Gorm the Old established the Danish monarchy, and the country has continued as a monarchy in one form or another ever since.

European Union—Denmark

The Monarchy

King Gorm the Old was succeeded by his son King Harald Bluetooth, who ruled from 950 to 985. King Harald's rule is recorded on the famous Jelling Stone. Sometimes referred to as Denmark's birth certificate, the enormous stone features a depiction of Jesus on the cross and has a runic inscription carved on its side. The stone states that King Harald converted the Danes to Christianity. In fact, the Danes did begin to convert to Roman Catholicism around this time. Denmark remained Roman Catholic until the **Protestant Reformation** occurred in neighboring Germany in the early 1500s. At that time, Denmark became predominantly Lutheran, and it remains so to this day.

Denmark continued to be ruled by Harald's descendants until the last king of the line died without an heir in 1448. At this time the monarch was chosen by an election limited to the royal family, though not to males only. In 1448, Count Christian of Old-enborg was elected king of Denmark under the name Christian I. His direct successors from the House of Oldenborg adopted alternately the names of Frederik and Christian, beginning with the election of Frederik I in 1523. The **elective** monarchy continued until 1660, when Frederik III decreed a **hereditary** monarchy for Denmark and Norway, which at the time was also under his rule.

Perhaps the most beloved monarch in Danish history was King Christian IV, memorialized today in the Danish national anthem. Although the anthem portrays King Christian as a victorious warrior, in truth he lost as many battles as he won. Fortunately, his greatest legacy is not his military record, but rather his lavish support of the arts and architecture. Throughout King Christian's reign, he contributed enormously to the development of Danish architecture, painting, music, and commerce. Many of Denmark's magnificent Renaissance buildings would not have existed without the financial support of the king.

Danish Nationalism and the Constitution

By 1806, the French general Napoleon Bonaparte had dissolved Germany's Holy Roman Empire completely and was working to expand his own empire across Europe. The defeat awakened a sense of **nationalism** in many European nations, prompting discussions of **linguistic** and cultural awareness throughout the people of Europe. It also renewed cries for political freedom and democracy that had begun with the revolution in the United States, and closer to home with the overthrow of the French monarchy.

These new political ideas had resonance for the Danish people, who were among the most prosperous and best educated of all the people in Europe at that time. Political parties began to form, and a movement began to give the Danish people a voice in their government, establishing basic **civil liberties** for all citizens.

In 1848, Denmark's Liberal Party called on King Frederik VII to renounce the system of **absolute monarchy** and form a democratically elected national assembly, which would then draft a **constitution** to establish the rights of all Danish citizens. The resulting constitution was signed into force on June 5, 1849, and was extremely **liberal** for its time. Overnight, Denmark became the most democratic and free nation in Europe. Unfortunately, the constitution was difficult to enforce, mostly because the king was not willing to give up his power. In the end, the entire monarchy was reconstructed, and Danish citizens received many basic rights, which they still possess.

In the years that followed, the new system of government led to widespread changes in Danish society. Peasants and men of great wealth and education were now equal under the law, and soon the common people were holding elected office. Women were granted full **suffrage** in 1915. Denmark remained **neutral** throughout World War I, although it did suffer an economic decline as many of its most important trading partners were embroiled in the conflict.

By 1924, **socialism** had become a prominent force in Denmark's political life, and in that year the Social Democrats became the nation's largest political party, a distinction they retained until 2001. During the Great Depression of the 1930s, the Social Democrats worked with local businesspeople to overcome some of the economic difficulties of the period, which also helped the party to gain more mainstream acceptance. Much of the legislation that would be the foundation for the modern **welfare state** present in Denmark today was passed during this period.

WORLD WAR II

By 1933, Adolph Hitler had come to power in nearby Germany, and by 1938, he had occupied neighboring Austria as well. His stated objective was to unify all ethnic German peoples. He soon demanded the surrender of Czechoslovakia's Sudetenland, taking up the cause of the Sudeten Germans. On September 29, 1938, France, Germany, Italy, and Great Britain signed the Munich Agreement, demanding that Czechoslovakia surrender the Sudetenland to Germany in exchange for a promise of peace. However, in March 1939, Hitler **reneged** on his agreement and invaded the remainder of Czechoslovakia. When it became clear that Hitler's aggression could not be stopped through negotiation and diplomacy, other nations had little choice but to declare war. Soon, much of the world was drawn in to the conflict.

Denmark once again proclaimed its neutrality, just as it had during World War I, but this time it could not evade involvement in the war. As a nation sharing much of Germany's northern border, Hitler could not allow Denmark to escape his control. On April 9, 1940, German forces invaded Denmark. Although thirty-nine Danish soldiers died during the invasion, the government ordered a halt to all resistance very early on, hoping to negotiate

The queen's residence, Freoensborg Palace

generous terms for the **occupation**. This approach was successful, as a cooperative Danish government meant that the Germans did not have to allocate manpower to oversee the daily affairs of the Danes.

In terms of Nazi race ideology, the Danes were fellow **Aryans**; the Nazis therefore considered the Danes more trustworthy than the Poles and the Slavs who inhabited other Nazi-occupied territories. As a result, the Danes were allowed to retain their democratically elected government, and many areas of life were largely unaffected by the occupation. Because relations with the Danes were so good, Nazi officials did not impose the restrictions on Danish Jews that it imposed in other areas, fearing a backlash from the general population. However, as the occupation continued, many Danes became disenchanted with Nazi control and an armed resistance movement formed.

Episodes of resistance, both in the form of violent acts of sabotage and in nonviolent civil disturbances, increased to the point that the Nazis dissolved the Danish government. In August 1943, **martial law** was implemented. Shortly afterward, resistance workers learned of a plan to remove all Danish Jews to **concentration camps** in Czechoslovakia. Thousands of everyday Danish citizens worked together to smuggle their Jewish neighbors out of the country in advance of the Nazi operation.

Fishermen built secret compartments in their boats to hide Jews on the short trip to neutral Sweden. Small children and the sick and infirm who could not make the journey were given Danish names and hidden in orphanages and senior-citizen homes. Nazi soldiers began to suspect what was happening and used police dogs trained to find hidden people. To throw the dogs off, chemists in Sweden concocted a mixture of dried rabbit's blood and cocaine, placing it on handkerchiefs. These were distributed to the fishermen. When a dog detected the presence of the rabbit's blood, he would sniff the handkerchief, and the cocaine would temporarily disable its sense of smell.

Of the nation's estimated 8,000 Jews, only 450 were captured by the Nazis and sent to concentration camps. Of those, fifty-one died before the war's end. The swift action on the part of the Danish people no doubt saved thousands of lives. Historians have called the event "the largest episode of mass **altruism** in history."

Denmark was eventually liberated from Nazi occupation in 1945. Although Denmark was spared many of the horrors of the conflict, there was still a significant loss of life, and the years immediately following the war were marked by economic hardship.

POSTWAR DEVELOPMENTS AND THE DENMARK OF TODAY

The years following World War II saw further political reform in Denmark. With the signing of a new constitution, the *Landsting*—the elected upper house of **parliament**—was abolished, and the female right of succession to the throne was guaranteed. After the war, with the perceived threat posed by

City Hall in Copenhagen

the Soviet Union and the lessons of World War II still fresh in Danish minds, the country abandoned its policy of neutrality.

Denmark became a charter member of the United Nations and was one of the founding members of the North Atlantic Treaty Organisation (NATO). Denmark had originally tried to form a defense alliance only with Norway and Sweden. As a result, the Nordic Council was later set up to coordinate policy between the three Nordic countries. In 1973, Danes voted yes to joining the European Community, the predecessor of the EU. Since then, Denmark has been a reluctant member of the European Community, opting out of many proposals, including the adoption of the euro as the national currency, which was rejected in a **referendum** in 2000. By 2007, however, many Danish leaders favored adopting the euro—but the decision was put off due the economic crisis that began in 2008.

In the twenty-first century, Denmark has participated in major military and humanitarian operations, most notably the UN- and NATO-led operations in Cyprus, Bosnia and Herzegovina, Korea, Egypt, Croatia, Kosovo, Ethiopia, Iraq, Afghanistan, and Somalia. Denmark held the EU presidency during the first half of 2012; priorities included promoting a responsible, green, and safe Europe, while working to steer Europe out of its economic crisis. For such a small country, Denmark continues to play a very large role in the global world!

Frederiksborg Castle brings the tourism industry to Denmark.

3 THE ECONOMY

Denmark is able to maintain its high standard of living due to the relative strength of its economy. Although recent economic downturns in other parts of Europe have affected the Danish economy, the country has still maintained a small margin of economic growth. The nation's well-developed *infrastructure*, highly educated and well-paid workforce, and *progressive* energy policies have all helped to develop the strong **market economy** that thrives in Denmark today.

THE NEW ECONOMY

As is happening in many **industrialized** nations, a shift has been made away from manufacturing as the primary source of economic growth. Although nearly one-third of Denmark's **gross domestic product (GDP)** still comes from its manufacturing enterprises, the dominant source of Denmark's income today comes from the **service sector**, which contributes 77 percent of the country's GDP. This includes the country's robust shipping industry, as well as the emerging sectors of **information technology** and tourism.

INDUSTRY

Denmark has a developed industrial economy. Despite the country's small size, the manufacturing sector in Denmark is very diverse and produces a variety of high-quality goods, both for export and for domestic consumption. Meat-processing factories, cigarette factories, dairies, corn mills, and breweries are among the most important of the food, beverage, and tobacco industries. Petroleum, insulin, and plastic goods are the main products produced by the Danish chemical industry.

From the nation's booming mechanical engineering businesses come motors, agricultural machines, pumps, thermostats, refrigerators, and telecommunications equipment. Finally, furniture, clothing, and toys are among the Danish industrial products sold in the greatest numbers. Major structural changes among the different areas of trade have brought new developments within the manufacturing sector. The manufacture of mechanical engineering products, which also include electronic goods, represents a growing proportion of the sector's productive value. The same applies to the chemical industry.

In contrast, the food, beverage, and tobacco industries have had a more or less constant share of production, whereas the textile, clothing, and leather industries have clearly been in decline. This can be attributed to increased competition from Third World countries and, more recently, the new EU member countries of central and eastern Europe, who can produce similar goods much less expensively due to the greater availability of raw materials and cheap labor.

AGRICULTURE

Danish agriculture produces enough food each year to feed 15 million people, which is almost three times the tiny nation's total population. Although the importance of agriculture in the Danish economy overall has fallen steadily with the rise of industrialization and the tremendous growth of the services sector, it is still an essential occupation due to its effect on employment and its importance in supplying everyday foodstuffs. As agricultural land accounts for almost two-thirds of the total area of the country, the industry is also important because of its impact on both the cultural and the scenic landscapes.

Farming in Denmark today is largely governed by the agricultural policies laid down by the EU, whose member countries are guaranteed a sale price for their agricultural goods that is better than that of the world market, regardless of whether sales are to the **domestic** market, the EU, or to

Traditional windmill in Skagen, Denmark

markets outside the EU. The support Danish farmers receive from the EU has helped make the country's agriculture one of the most sophisticated agricultural regions in the whole world. Farming methods in Denmark have been developed and implemented to prevent negative envi-

the end consumer with a safe and wholesome food supply. As a result, Denmark has benefited greatly from the EU agricultural policy.

ENERGY

Denmark's holdings in the North Sea produce more oil and natural gas than is needed domestically. This has resulted in energy becoming a vital export. Oil and gas are taken ashore, then distributed and exported via pipelines. Gas is exported to Sweden and Germany, while the surplus oil is mainly sold to a variety of countries. Denmark is the third-largest oil producer in Western Europe, after Norway and Great Britain. Together with gas production, the nation's oil wealth is an important reason why Denmark has had an energy surplus for the last two decades.

Electricity is mainly produced in regional power stations by burning coal supplemented with natural gas, oil, biological fuel, and waste products. Natural gas is playing an increasingly important role, while the use of oil is decreasing. Most heating energy is currently produced in the home. Technology used in homes and offices for heating

---

QUICK FACTS: THE ECONOMY OF DENMARK

Gross Domestic Product (GDP): US$208.8 billion (2011 est.)

GDP per capita: US$40,200 (2011 est.)

Industries: iron, steel, nonferrous metals, chemicals, food processing, machinery and transportation equipment, textiles and clothing, electronics, construction, furniture and other wood products, shipbuilding and refurbishment, windmills, pharmaceuticals, medical equipment

Agriculture: barley, wheat, potatoes, sugar beets; pork, dairy products; fish

Export commodities: machinery and instruments, meat and meat products, dairy products, fish, pharmaceuticals, furniture, windmills

Export partners: Germany 17.6%, Sweden 13.8%, UK 8.1%, US 5.9%, Norway 5.6%, Netherlands 4.8%, France 4.7% (2010)

Import commodities: machinery and equipment, raw materials and semi-manufactures for industry, chemicals, grain and foodstuffs, consumer goods

Import partners: Germany 21.1%, Sweden 13.7%, Netherlands 7.3%, China 6.8%, UK 6.1%, Norway 5.5% (2010)

Currency: Danish krone (DKK)

Currency exchange rate: US$1 =5.291 DKK (March 2012 est.)

Note: All figures are from 2011 unless otherwise noted.
Source: www.cia.gov, 2012.

---

ronmental impact, decrease the use of pesticides, conserve energy, and most important, provide

The waterfront in Copenhagen

include oil and gas boilers, straw- and wood-burning stoves, solar energy, ground heat, and **geothermal** heating systems. Until recently, oil-burning furnaces in individual homes were the traditional Danish form of heating, but their numbers are falling, and domestic heating is being replaced by other methods. Only in rural districts is oil included in heating plans for the future.

Natural gas pipelines have been taken to most homes in the more densely populated areas. There is no obligation to be connected to the pipelines, but the Danish people have a strong sense that it is important to do one's part for the environment—so most families are making a switch.

Individual consumption of energy is much lower in Denmark than in most industrialized nations.

The krone is the Danish currency unit.

Conservation of energy plays an important role in energy planning. A government program was introduced to promote insulation of Danish homes; as a result, nearly all homes have now been insulated. A heating inspection is required when houses are sold. In addition, citizens are encouraged by information campaigns and grants to conserve energy. These programs have been very successful, as Denmark has been able to maintain its energy consumption at the same level for the last several years.

TRANSPORTATION

Denmark has 44,669 miles (71,888 km.) of road and 1,720 miles (2,768 km.) of railway, 291 railway stations and goods terminals, 124 ports, and 23 airports. Most people travel by car in Denmark. In recent years, car and railway traffic has increased as more bridges have been built between Denmark's many islands, while ferry and domestic flight traffic has decreased. Most goods transported domestically are carried by Danish trucks, while most goods transported internationally are carried by ship. Only a limited number are transported by train and very few by plane.

LOOKING TO THE FUTURE

Denmark looks forward to continued prosperity, although a few concerns do exist. The nation's elaborate welfare system is a significant drain on the economy, and the high taxes imposed on Danish citizens and corporations make the country less competitive in some respects as it competes with the emerging democracies in Central and Eastern Europe for foreign investment. Unemployment has also been very high over the last decade, although recent legislation seems to have corrected that problem to a large extent. Overall, the economic forecast for Denmark continues to look very bright.

ECONOMIC CRISIS

Unfortunately, Denmark's reluctance to become entangled with the changing world economy did not save this nation from the world recession that began in 2008. The economic crisis hit Denmark just as hard as it did other nations. Denmark's economy depends on trade with the rest of the world—and with the rest of the world staggering financially, Denmark's trade was bound to drop.

Although Denmark previously had a relatively low unemployment rate, now it nearly doubled in only a short time. There were no longer enough jobs to go around. Unemployment is expected to rise even more within the next few years. Denmark, like the rest of the world, must find its way through the crisis, although it has faired better than many other EU members.

Luckily, Denmark is a very technologically advanced, developed nation with a good safety net for the problems that lie ahead. Health care is available to anyone, no matter what economic situation they are in. Although these areas have suffered, they are still there to help Danes survive the current crisis.

Mime performers at Tivoli Palace

4 DENMARK'S PEOPLE AND CULTURE

Denmark, home to more than 5 million people, is a small but vibrant country. Although the country's population includes 400,000 citizens of foreign origin, Denmark is generally considered to be ethnically and religiously **homogeneous**. Danish is the national language. An ancient language, Danish is related to both German and the old Viking tongue. Many Danish words are used in more than one way.

For instance, *hej* means "hello," but *hej hej* means "goodbye." The pronunciation of Danish is difficult for nonnative speakers because the consonants are often barely enunciated, which makes them difficult for the untrained listener to detect.

The structure of the traditional Danish family has undergone some changes in the last few decades. Today, it is normal for a couple to live together for many years in what is known as a "paperless marriage." It is also considered normal for couples to have children without being wed, and many women keep their maiden names after they are married, which means that Danish children often inherit two last names. Same-sex couples in Denmark may register their domestic partnerships, giving them the same legal rights as a

Traditional half-timbered Danish house near Lejre, Zealand

married heterosexual couple. Although same-sex couples cannot be married in church, the Lutheran church gives them its blessing.

THE WELFARE STATE

Since the creation of the so-called welfare state in the 1970s, Denmark has boasted one of the highest standards of living in the world. Its programs include a highly developed social security system, which guarantees that no one will suffer a serious decline in their standard of living due to illness or unemployment. In addition, anyone aged sixty-seven or older is entitled to an old-age pension, and all citizens can access free health care. All Danish students have the right to a free education, including studies at the university level. Naturally, the cost of these programs is considerable, and the Danish people currently pay one of the highest levels of income tax in the world to finance these social programs.

RELIGION: FREEDOM OF CHOICE

All Danish citizens enjoy complete freedom of religion, and the law protects the right of citizens to wor-ship freely. The official religion of Denmark is the Lutheran faith, and nearly 90 percent of Danes are baptized into the Lutheran Evangelical Church. The second-largest religious faith in Denmark is Islam, owing to the large numbers of immigrants who have made their way to Denmark in recent decades from the countries of the Middle East and North Africa. A number of smaller Christian churches are represented in Denmark, and they have been accorded the status of officially recognized religious communities. These include the Roman Catholic Church, the Danish Baptist Church, the Pentecostal Church, the Seventh Day Adventists, the Catholic Apostolic Church, the Salvation Army, the Methodist Church, the Anglican Church, and the Russian Orthodox Church.

FOOD AND DRINK: THE TRADITIONAL COLD BUFFET

The heart of the Danish diet does not lie with any one particular dish but rather in the whole idea and presentation of the cold buffet. The basic elements are bread, cold meat, fish, or cheese, and the condiments placed on top of other items. Not just any combination will do, however. Certain meats and cheeses are used exclusively with certain breads. The bread is either rye or white and is always eaten buttered. The most common sandwiches are smoked herring topped with egg yolk, radishes, and chives; smoked eel with scrambled eggs; pork with red cabbage, apples, and prunes;

or liverwurst with pickles. The most common way for Danes to eat lunch is the *madpakken*, where open-faced sandwiches are specially wrapped in wax paper. Thus, lunch is available at work or school with a minimum of fuss.

Quick Facts: The People of Denmark

Population: 5,543,453 (July 2012 est.)
Ethnic groups: Scandinavian, Inuit, Faroese, German, Turkish, Iranian, Somali
Age structure:
  0–14 years: 17.6%
  15–64 years: 65.3%
  65 years and above: 17.1% (2011 est.)
Population growth rate: 0.239% (2012 est.)
Birth rate: 10.22 births/1,000 population (2012 est.)
Death rate: 10.19 deaths/1,000 population (July 2012 est.)
Migration rate: 2.36 migrant(s)/1,000 population (2012 est.)
Infant mortality rate: 4.56 deaths/1,000 live births
Life expectancy at birth:
  Total population: 77.62 years
  Male: 75.34 years
  Female: 80.03 years
Total fertility rate: 4.19 deaths/1,000 live births
Religions: Evangelical Lutheran (official) 95%, other Christian (includes Protestant and Roman Catholic) 3%, Muslim 2%
Languages: Danish, Faroese, Greenlandic (an Inuit dialect), German (small minority)
Literacy rate: 99%

Note: All figures are from 2011.
Source: www.cia.gov, 2012.

EDUCATION AND SPORTS: A LITERATE AND ACTIVE PEOPLE

Danes take both education and sports very seriously. Almost all adults can read and write, and most can speak at least one foreign language; many speak two. The country has produced great thinkers and sports figures.

Education is compulsory in Denmark. Virtually all children in Denmark attend public schools. and all public schools are free. Less than 10 percent of Danish students choose to attend private schools, which require that private tuition be paid by a student's parents. Attending a college or university is also free in Denmark, with students receiving government grants on a monthly basis.

Soccer—or football, as it is known in Europe—is Denmark's national sport, but swimming, sailing, cycling, and cross-country running are also very popular, both as spectator sports and as pastimes for all citizens. A growing number of people now go jogging in the morning or evening. Denmark has won Olympic gold medals in handball, sailing, riding, shooting, swimming, rowing, tug-of-war, and cycling.

Denmark's most famous author, Hans Christian Andersen

Karen Blixen's study in Rungstedlund

The Dannebrog: A Symbol of Pride

Denmark's red-and-white flag is the *Dannebrog*, "flag of the Danes." Legend has it that the Dannebrog fell from the sky on June 15, 1219, as God's way of inspiring the Danish forces during a particularly bloody battle.

Danes fly their flag with pride. People in rural areas often have their own flagpole set squarely in the middle of their garden. On holidays and birthdays, miniature flags are used as table decorations, and Christmas trees are traditionally trimmed with miniature versions of the flag. Use of the Danish flag has also become important in advertising and promoting domestically produced products in the marketplace. Danish soccer fans are proud of the fact that they were the first fans to paint their faces and bodies with their flag in support of the national soccer team. Unlike the displays sometimes seen in other countries, to display the flag in Denmark is not a sign of nationalism but rather a long-standing cultural custom.

Famous Danes

Danish society has produced many important thinkers, artists, and scientists. Danes are very proud of the contributions made by some of their famous citizens.

Hans Christian Andersen, born on the island of Funen to a shoemaker and a washerwoman, wrote fanciful fairytales that have been a source of delight to children and adults throughout the world. A statue of the Little Mermaid, one of Andersen's most beloved characters, is now one of Copenhagen's biggest tourist attractions.

Søren Kierkegaard was also a famous writer, although his subject matter was a little more serious. A notable philosopher, Kierkegaard wrote many books on Christianity and the philosophical problems of modern existence.

Karen Blixen invented the pseudonym Isak Dinesen and went on to use it for most of her writing career. For many years she lived in Kenya, where her most famous novel, *Out of Africa*, was written. Today, tourists can visit both the farm she lived on in Kenya and her house in Rungsted, Denmark.

The nation has also produced great scientists. Nobel Prize–winning physicist Niels Bohr was one of Denmark's most famous scientists. Bohr was one of the fathers of atomic energy and also helped to organize the periodic table. A brilliant researcher and one of the most prominent personalities in modern science, he was also very outspoken about the consequences and ethical implications of the invention of the nuclear bomb.

Nyhavn Copenhagen

5 LOOKING TO THE FUTURE

L ike the rest of the world, Denmark has many problems to solve. Immigration issues, terrorism, financial crises, prejudice, and political conflicts are challenges that face most of the world's countries, and Denmark is no exception.

Denmark gets 20 percent of its electricity from wind farms like these ones in Jutland, Denmark.

What Denmark has going for it is a well-educated population who possess many resources. Hopefully, these strengths will allow the Danes to find ways to overcome their challenges and emerge in the future even stronger.

ENVIRONMENTAL ADVANCEMENTS

One of Denmark's greatest strengths is the way it is protecting the environment for the future. Denmark was one of the world's first nations to wake up to the dangers of foreign oil dependence after the 1973 Arab **embargo**. At that time, oil, almost all of it imported, met 90 percent of the country's energy. Denmark's leaders immediately responded by putting their nation on a path toward energy independence.

New homes in Denmark today are twice as energy efficient as they were before the oil embargo. What's more, waste heat from local power plants heats Denmark's homes and offices. Denmark's taxes on new cars and motor fuel are among the highest in Europe, which has encouraged Danes to find other ways to get around. In Copenhagen, a third of commuters travel by bike. The average Dane uses less than half as much energy every year than does the average American!

Denmark is also committed to wind energy. Since 1979, the Danish government has supported wind farms, and today, Denmark gets 20 percent of its electricity from wind energy. The country's wind industry employs about 26,000 people, nearly 1 percent of the workforce, and wind energy accounts for 7 percent of Denmark's export income. Government leaders and utility executives expect wind to provide fully half of the country's electricity by the 2020s. To reach this goal, Denmark is looking to new offshore wind projects. Even cars will soon be able to plug into this totally clean source of power, recharging during low-demand nighttime hours when Denmark's winds continue to blow.

DENMARK AND THE UNITED STATES

Denmark's relationship with the United States has been good for a long time. These two countries have worked together for decades, and the United States is currently Denmark's largest trade partner outside of Europe. American culture has had a strong influence on Denmark, especially when it comes to music and television. Many tourists from the United States find their way to Denmark throughout the year.

As the world becomes more intimately connected, the relationship Denmark has with the United States will only continue to grow. Hopefully, America will be most inspired by Denmark's commitment to the environment. If the United States and countries around the globe can learn from Denmark's example, the world's future will be far brighter!

Time Line

3000 BCE	Denmark's earliest inhabitants settle along the coast.
500 CE	The Danes invade from neighboring Sweden and conquer the area.
800	Godfred the Viking establishes Denmark's boundaries and repels the Franks.
900	Gorm the Old establishes the Danish monarchy.
950	King Harald Bluetooth begins to convert Denmark to Christianity.
1448	Count Christian of Oldenborg is elected King of Denmark under the name Christian I.
1660	King Frederik III decrees a hereditary monarchy for Denmark and Norway.
1848	Denmark's Liberal Party calls on King Frederik VII to renounce the system of absolute monarchy.
1849	The Danish Constitution is signed into law.
1914	World War I begins; Denmark remains neutral.
1915	Women are granted the right to vote.
1924	The Democratic Socialist Party becomes Denmark's largest political party.
1940	Nazi Germany invades Denmark.
1943	The Nazi's institute martial law; Danish Jews are smuggled into neutral Sweden.
1945	Denmark is liberated from Nazi occupation by the Allies.
1945	Denmark becomes a charter member of the United Nations.
1949	Denmark becomes a founding member of NATO.
1952	Denmark forms the Nordic Council with Finland, Iceland, Norway, and Sweden.
1953	Many political changes are implemented including the abolition of the upper house of parliament and legal establishment of the female right of succession.
1957	The European Economic Community begins between Germany, France, Belgium, Italy, Luxembourg, and the Netherlands.
1973	Denmark joins the EEC along with Great Britain.
1992	The Maastricht Treaty is signed, creating the EU; Denmark initially rejects the treaty.
1993	A second Danish referendum ratifies the Maastricht Treaty.
2000	Denmark rejects a proposal to adopt the euro as its national currency.
2005	Danish newspaper prints cartoon of the Prophet Mohammed, which incites Muslim protests around the world.
2008	Global economic recession begins.
2010	Danish government proposes tighter immigration laws that would go into effect in 2011.
2012	Denmark holds the EU presidency during the first half of the year.

FURTHER READING/INTERNET RESOURCES

Deedy, Carmen Agra, and Henri Sorensen. *The Yellow Star: The Legend of King Christian X of Denmark*. Atlanta, Ga.: Peachtree Publishers, 2000.
Murphy, Patrick J. *Denmark*. Mankato, Minn.: Capstone Press, 2002.
Pateman, Robert. *Denmark*. Salt Lake City, Utah: Benchmark Books, 2005.
Stein, Conrad. *Denmark*. New York: Children's Press, 2003.
Wild, Mary C. *Denmark*. New York: Thomas Gale, 2004.

Travel Information
www.lonelyplanet.com/destinations/europe/denmark
www.dt.dk

History and Geography
www.infoplease.com
www.wikipedia.org

Culture and Festivals
www.denmark.dk
www.um.dk

Economic and Political Information
www.cia.gov
www.wikipedia.org

EU Information
europa.eu.int

FOR MORE INFORMATION

Danish Embassy
3200 Whitehaven St. NW
Washington, DC 20008
Tel.: 202-234-4300
Fax: 202-328-1470

Embassy of the United States in Copenhagen
Dag Hammarskjölds Allé 24
2100 Copenhagen Ø
Denmark
e-mail: mail@usembassy.dk

European Union
Delegation of the European Commission to the United States
2300 M Street, NW
Washington, DC 20037
Tel.: 202-862-9500
Fax: 202-429-1766

GLOSSARY

absolute monarchy: A system of government in which a king or queen has total power and authority.

altruism: An attitude or way of behaving characterized by unselfish concern for the welfare of others.

Aryans: In Nazi thought, Caucasians of non-Semitic descent regarded as racially superior.

autonomous: Self-governing.

bogs: Areas of wet, marshy ground, consisting primarily of decomposing plant material.

civil liberties: The basic rights guaranteed to individual citizens by law.

concentration camps: Prison camps used for exterminating prisoners under the rule of Hitler in Nazi Germany.

constitution: The written principles and laws by which a country is governed.

democratic: the form of government where power is held by the people, and exercised through a system of representation involving free elections.

discrimination: Unfair treatment because of race, religion, sex, or some other difference.

domestic: Having to do with or originating from ones own country.

elective: Chosen by a vote.

embargo: A ban on trade with a particular country.

geothermal: Using the heat of the earth's interior to produce energy.

gross domestic product (GDP): The total market value of all the goods and services produced by a nation during a specified period.

hereditary: Handed down through generations by inheritance.

homogeneous: Having a uniform composition or structure.

industrialized: Adapted a country or group to industrial methods of production and manufacturing.

inflammatory: Intended to make people angry.

information technology: The use of technologies such as computing and telecommunications to process and distribute information in digital and other forms.

infrastructure: A country's large-scale public systems, services, and facilities that are necessary for economic activity.

liberal: Tolerant of different views and standards of behavior.

linguistic: Relating to languages.

market economy: An economy where prices and wages are determined mainly by the market and the laws of supply and demand rather than government regulations.

martial law: The control and policing of a civilian population by military forces and according to military rules.

nationalism: A strong sense of pride in one's country.

neutral: Not taking sides in a conflict.

occupation: The invasion of a country or region by enemy forces.

pagan: An ancient multigod religion.

parliament: A nation's legislative body.

prejudice: Fear or hatred of a particular group.

progressive: Progressing gradually over a period of time.

Protestant Reformation: The sixteenth-century religious movement intended to reform the Roman Catholic Church, which led instead to the formation of Protestantism.

radicals: People who take an extreme position.

referendum: A vote by the whole of an electorate on a specific question or questions put to it by a government.

reneged: Went back on a promise or pledge.

runic: Characteristic of a character in any of several ancient Germanic alphabets.

service sector: The part of the economy that provides services rather than products.

socialism: A political system in which the means of production and distribution are controlled by the people and operated based on fairness, not market principles.

solidarity: The act of standing together, presenting a united front.

sufferage: The right to vote in elections.

welfare state: A nation whose government assumes primary responsibility for the social welfare of its citizens.

INDEX

agriculture 38–40
ancient Denmark 25–28
Andersen, Hans Christian 51

Blixen, Karen 51
Bohr, Niels 51

Christianity 14, 18, 28, 29, 47, 51
climate 21
Common Agricultural Policy (CAP) 40
the constitution 29–30
Copenhagen 16, 18, 27, 51, 55

Danes 10, 12, 16, 18, 25, 26, 29, 32, 43, 47, 48, 51, 54, 55
democracy 29

economy 13, 37–43
    agriculture 38–39
    energy 40–43
    the future 43
    industry 38
    new economy 38
    transportation 43
education 47, 48
the environment 54–55
euro 11, 13, 35
European Union 11–13, 21, 14

food and drink 47–48
Franks 26
    Charlemagne 26

geography 21
Great Depression 30
Gypsies 17–18

Immigration 16, 21, 23, 54, 56
information technology 38

Kierkegaard, Søren 51

language 18, 21, 25, 26, 45, 48

monarchy 28–30
Muslim 13–16

nationalism 29–30, 51

Protestant Reformation 29

religion 14, 47, 48
Roma 17–18, 21

shipping industry 38
socialism 30
social security system 47
sports 48

tourism 38

Vikings 26–28

welfare 30, 43, 47
World War II 13, 30, 32, 35

PICTURE CREDITS

About the Authors and the Consultant

Authors

Heather Docalavich first developed an interest in the history and cultures of Eastern Europe through her work as a genealogy researcher. She currently resides in Hilton Head, South Carolina, with her four children.

Shaina Carmel Indovino is a writer and illustrator living in Nesconset, New York. She graduated from Binghamton University, where she received degrees in sociology and English. Shaina has enjoyed the opportunity to apply both of her fields of study to her writing and she hopes readers will benefit from taking a look at the countries of the world through more than one perspective.

Series Consultant

Ambassador John Bruton served as Irish Prime Minister from 1994 until 1997. As prime minister, he helped turn Ireland's economy into one of the fastest-growing in the world. He was also involved in the Northern Ireland Peace Process, which led to the 1998 Good Friday Agreement. During his tenure as Ireland's prime minister, he also presided over the European Union presidency in 1996 and helped finalize the Stability and Growth Pact, which governs management of the euro. Before being named the European Commission Head of Delegation in the United States, he was a member of the convention that drafted the European Constitution, signed October 29, 2004.

The European Commission Delegation to the United States represents the interests of the European Union as a whole, much as ambassadors represent their countries' interests to the U.S. government. Matters coming under European Commission authority are negotiated between the commission and the U.S. administration.